WHAT THE F*CK ARE WE THINKING?

ANONYMOUS

Tellwell Talent
www.tellwell.ca

ISBN
978-0-2288-5255-1 (Paperback)
978-0-2288-5256-8 (eBook)

Acknowledgements

This book is for all of you. I'm hoping that you will make use of this book to inspire some change for this planet of ours. And for my best friend who left this world far too soon. I really miss talking with you about this stuff.

Table of Contents

Foreword

What are we doing? Are we all content with the direction that our global society is headed? Do you feel like you have some good ideas on how to change things, but you have no idea how to get your voice heard? There are wonderful ideas out there, and many of you are expressing them in your own way. There are countless books targeting the improvement of your health. There are many religions whose purpose should be to help us to connect with our conceptions of God. There are inspirational songs, movies, poems, videos, and artworks that invite us to experience the spiritual. There are communities everywhere that are encouraging us to help one another. People are waking up. People want to change.

The problem is, in order to access these things, we have to be watching the right movies, listening to the right songs, reading the right books, or hearing the right people. It is a difficult thing to do when we are all so divided. It is even more difficult when people don't have access to these technologies. What if we were to find a way to come together? What if we were to find a way to get everyone access to technology?

There are intelligent people out there pleading with us to change. They are writing songs, writing books, and creating podcasts or internet videos. They have amazing ideas, and they are trying to reach the population. The trouble with all of these different perspectives on how we should change is that there is no connection between them. To get behind any of them, not only do we have to watch the right movies, listen to the right songs, read the right books, and hear the right people, but we also have to agree with them. The issue here is that there are so many different opinions among all of us, it is impossible to get everyone to come to any kind of global agreement on anything. For every opinion, there is an equal and opposite opinion.

Are there really any recognizable global communication platforms out there that will tolerate differences of opinion? Is there a way for us all to get our ideas heard without judgment? What if we were to create one? At the end of this book, I will provide you with some contact information. I want to hear from you. I want to discuss your ideas on how we can go about changing the world. I want to get your ideas heard.

As this book gains a following and any consequent financial success, the goal is to create a platform for our discussion. We can create podcasts, organize interviews and talks, write follow-up books, or even create television or radio programming to forward our ideas. But I will need your help.

What if this book were to inspire a global revolution? One that invites every single one of you to become a part of it. What if our revolution were to tolerate everyone's differences in opinion? What if we could create a forum where all of our voices could be heard? None of us are perfect, but what if we could somehow manage to point ourselves in the same direction when it comes to the preservation of our planet? The preservation of our humanity?

If you are easily offended, this book might not be for you. But then again, can you be challenged to go ahead and be offended, then read on anyway? Can we assume that if you've opened this book, you aren't someone with the shortest of fuses? Including the word "fuck" in the title should weed out some of the easily offended. Even those of you who consider yourselves individuals blessed with open-mindedness—I am going to test your resolve.

I invite you to use that brain of yours. There will be far more questions than answers. We are all intelligent creatures. My purpose is to write a book that will become a symbol for change.

The perspectives contained in this book could easily be explored in much further detail. I'm hoping that one day they will be, but I would rather explore them with you.

The timing of a book's release is paramount to its success. There has never been a more opportune moment than the present. People everywhere are waking up. People are starting to ask some of these questions for themselves. People want to change, but they aren't quite sure how to go about it. We need some direction.

If this book were to hold your attention for its entirety, my hope is that we will come away from it with a real desire for some direction. I'm hoping you will want to take this thing even further. If you have ideas on how we might do that, I want to hear from you.

In no way does this book demand that you adopt any of the perspectives contained within, but challenge yourself to tolerate them. Some will resonate with you, while some certainly will not. Be tolerant. If we manage to create a forum for the expressions of our ideas, the possibilities for change are endless.

The purpose of this book is to offer a perspective on how we might change our behaviour. I am not a professional writer, so please bear with me. I am average in every way. I am you. But I will challenge your ideas on some of our primary global concerns. This book will offer up perspective, while inviting you to add your own opinions to the discussion. This book is only the beginning. Read it, and then let's get together and talk about our future.

We are Offended

Do you look around and find yourself concerned for the future of our planet? Should we worry about what we've come to accept as the status quo in our global society? Have we lost our perspective? Shouldn't we be ashamed of what we are doing to this planet of ours? Shouldn't we question what we have decided is a perfectly acceptable planet for our children to inherit?

We have twisted up our ideas on religion, politics, and the diversity of wealth into misrepresentations of what we hoped things would look like. We are divided. Cancel culture is rampant. That means we have no tolerance for opinions and ideas that differ from our own. Things like politics, religion, social media, or even the news—they all feed off of our lack of tolerance. Politicians and their associated parties spend far more time throwing their rivals under the proverbial bus, instead of highlighting any sort of inclusive, less divisive ideologies that we can get behind. Don't our politicians seem to be far more concerned with attaining and maintaining power? Is that okay with you?

How many people are living on the planet today? Every person's opinions are based on their own experiences, their own belief systems, and their own ideologies. It isn't possible for any government to placate all of its citizens. Yet we expect them to do just that. All politics seem to do these days is set us up for all sorts of arguments over nothing more than our opinions. Politics thrives on our intolerance. Even in democratic nations, do the political parties not spend endless hours engaging us by highlighting what is wrong with their political rivals?

We see political parties, with their sole aspirations being to achieve and maintain power, spending much of their time trying to direct our anger toward their political opponents. They divide us. They use our intolerances to distract us from what is truly going on. There is an illusion of democracy. Are your governments even interested in the well-being of its citizens? Have we not just set up our governments to be far more concerned with their own well-being than with ours? They will manipulate us to fight civil or even global wars over our differences in political opinions. Aren't wars often fought in order to maintain the systems that keep our politicians rich and in control of things? Why do we see politicians entering their roles as average citizens, then leaving those roles as millionaires? Think about that for a moment. It's craziness.

Wouldn't you like to affect some change? Wouldn't you rather these political parties spend all of their time solely discussing what they intend to do for us, instead of stoking our anger over what they conceive to be wrong with their political rivals? Shouldn't we be more interested in how they are going to nurture a better society for you and me?

They are always going to find political support if they can simply get us to disagree with one another. If they can distract you and me by having us engage one another in petty arguments over differences in political opinion, aren't we less likely to focus on the issues that should actually concern us? We seem to be unaware that it is impossible for them to make every single one of us simultaneously happy. They are simply using our anger, our fear, and our intolerance against us for their benefit. We ignore their universal corruption.

Take a look at the government that represents you. Ask yourself, are you being manipulated or controlled by that government in any way? Then ask yourself, why you think that is? More importantly, ask yourself if your voice can really be heard if you were to demand change. If you live in certain parts of the world and are afraid of what might happen to you should you raise your voice to have your opinions heard, then there is a serious problem.

That is just politics. Why don't we challenge some of our ideas on all kinds of different topics? We have incorporated into our religious structures this idea that we must disbelieve in other religions. A shift in perspective here could change the world right now! We fight wars over this shit. Over and over again. Just open any history book and you will find this to be true.

Do you ever shut down when people start talking about religion? Why is that? We have this built-in intolerance when it comes to talking about this stuff. We seem to instinctively resort to this, "I am right, you are wrong" mentality. It isn't working, people. We are only escalating our propensity for division. It needs to stop. The only requirement is a simple, universal shift to a more tolerant perspective when it comes to those religious belief systems that differ from your own.

If we continue with our arguments over differences of opinion, we are quite literally going to blow ourselves up. History has foreshadowed this eventuality, and on a smaller scale, it has played out several times through war and conflict. Unfortunately, we seem oblivious to the lessons of our predecessors. Think about it for a moment. With all of the wars that have taken place on our planet, can you not imagine our ancestors, dressed in their military fatigues, crying on those battlefields, begging us to change our ways? Why are we so oblivious to their warnings? We seem to have this, "It won't happen to us, certainly not in our lifetimes" attitude hard-wired into our beings. We need a radical change in perspective here. We need to recognize that we are all the same. We are humans, and we need to stop destroying one another.

If the COVID-19 pandemic proved anything, it is that it can happen to us. Without a radical and immediate change in our world-wide perspectives, would you not agree that all kinds of catastrophe are inevitable? People will continue to suffer. We are divided on everything. We are full of hate. We are offended, and we lack tolerance for everyone and everything. Do we not want to change all of this?

So, what do we do about it? We can start by joining one another on a journey of discussion. What are the questions you would like to have answered? How would you shape your own questions to affect some change for the world? If we can all start thinking, talking, and better yet, feeling, wouldn't we be motivated to promote some shifts in the perspectives of our own ideologies? We can change.

It is time to create a new symbol for change, and you are all invited to become a part of that. It is time to begin world-wide discussion. We must develop a global platform for our discussions that will transcend political, religious, and economic boundaries. Shouldn't we be excited to explore any means by which we might come together as a global community? We will need to support one another. We have certainly found incalculable means by which to drive one another further apart. Why don't we simply stop doing that?

We can solve all of our problems by incorporating one simple idea into every aspect of our lives: Tolerance. It is the opposite of being offended. Do you think we are a tolerant lot? If not, then if we could just find a little bit of tolerance for differences in opinion, wouldn't we have a jumping off point for discussion? If we can bring ourselves to tolerate opinions that differ from our own, wouldn't we be setting ourselves up for discussion rather than confrontation? Wouldn't we be setting ourselves up for a more peaceful existence? We must stop being offended.

Tolerance for ideologies such as differences in political opinions, religious affiliations, sexual orientations, race, socio-economic backgrounds, social statuses, or even cultures are just a few examples of issues where we could explore more tolerant perspectives. What are your thoughts on abortion? How do you feel about capital punishment? Do you have an opinion on parenting methodologies? Do you support vaccinations? Are you in favor of diets that include animal meat? Do you support the fossil fuel industry? Would you like to see the planet leaning toward renewable energy? Where do you stand on addiction? Do you think that everyone on the planet is ever going to agree with all of your opinions? Do you think they should? Of course not. Wouldn't it be wonderful if we could talk about these things without fighting? All we have to do is abandon our belligerent intolerance. Most of us are trying to teach our children how to do just that.

Have any of these topics sparked any sort of emotional response within you? There aren't any wrong answers. The idea is to get us all thinking from a tolerant perspective. Can you allow your mind to open up sufficiently to consider those opinions that differ from your own? Can you listen without judgment, or would you rather fight to defend your point of view? If you find yourself wanting to fight, or if you are already planning a heated response to this book, I have just highlighted society's biggest problem. We live in a constant state of being offended. We seem to behave as though we have a complete and utter lack for the capacity to be tolerant. But if we refuse to find a way to be tolerant, aren't we are all so very screwed?

With tolerance as the underlying theme, we first need to start feeling better about ourselves. We can't help anybody else if we haven't found some peace within our own lives. There are innumerable methods by which to accomplish this. There are amazing people among us who will be our guides.

We will examine a few simple principles that will hopefully bring some serenity to your own existence. None of them are new ideas. There are so many "self-help" books out there. They have been written by people far more intelligent than I. We would be wise to read as many of them as we can.

There are many different perspectives on the spiritual. What if we were to choose to consider they may all have merit? The premise of religion is that anyone can choose what they want to believe in. If we want the freedom to choose what we want to believe in, then we must tolerate everyone else's freedom to choose, as well. If anyone has found a means to connect with their own concept of God, shouldn't we all be standing beside one another absolutely?

Take your newfound serenity and extend some kindness to your fellow human beings. Shouldn't we be promoting more peace and happiness among our fellow humans? Wouldn't you like to be a part of encouraging one another's thoughts and creativity? What if we could re-energize our spirits?

Whatever your opinions might be, challenge yourself to consider some of the ideas here before you are inclined to judge them. Should this book find its purpose, the great minds from every corner of the world will come together. We will discuss what we want our collective futures to look like. We might even save this planet of ours. This book is only a beginning. Challenge your own perspectives here. We have so much to talk about.

The Fear Wars

Consider war. Is there anything more predictable in human history than our propensity for war? What is war, really? Doesn't war originate out of our own intolerance or fear? Couldn't we say that one group of people within our society, for whatever reason, will not tolerate the opinions or behaviours of another group of people? Opposing groups begin to fear one another, and they nurture the precursors for war. I realize that this is a simplification of what war means, but please bear with me for a moment. For the sake of simplicity here, we do not need to dissect each and every conflict throughout human history. This is not our purpose.

Wars are often conflicts involving human sacrifice that do not necessarily represent the hopes and dreams of those doing the sacrificing. Aren't wars started because the individuals that we have placed in power are intolerant or fearful of something? Our leaders will pass their fears and intolerances onto us, and we start to believe that our way of living is in imminent jeopardy. We are so fearful that we become willing and able to kill one another in order to protect our own way of life. But is our way of life truly being threatened? If we could get rid of fear and intolerance, could we not do away with war altogether?

Aren't we being manipulated to fear that something might change? Aren't we often led to believe that our freedom, our property, our identity, our safety, or our families are going to be taken away from us? We become afraid, and we will fight. What if our intolerance and fear is being manipulated and amplified by someone holding some sort of power over us? Have our minds been twisted to believe that we must destroy before being destroyed? This is so ironic because we are taught to fear change, when change is exactly what we need to be striving toward.

Perhaps our leaders aren't wrong. Maybe some sort of freedom or possession is, in fact, about to be taken away from us. But if so, isn't it going be taken away from us by someone on the "other side" that has been similarly manipulated? If we were all to adopt a perspective of tolerance on both sides of the proverbial fence, wouldn't we be less likely inclined to fight one another? It all starts with tolerance. We need leaders that will promote this idea on a world-wide scale. Without tolerant leaders, "unfortunate" would be a drastic minimization of the events that have continued to transpire over time.

Imagine that you are led to believe that a different culture of people is about to take something away from you. Your home, your food, or your loved ones. Are you not already willing to fight? Kill even, should it come to that? But what if that culture actually has no intention of taking anything away from you? What if, for one reason or another, you have only been manipulated to believe this to be true? In this moment are you not prepared to fight for no reason whatsoever? Is that not an interesting phenomenon? It is a phenomenon of human nature that can be so easily manipulated or exploited by the powers that be.

By nature, we are fearful creatures. There is nothing wrong with that. Fear, in the right circumstances, keeps us alive. It is primal, it is instinctive, and in the right circumstances, our survival depends on it. But what is really happening in the world? We have divided ourselves with borders. We have divided ourselves by our ideologies. We have divided ourselves by religion, skin colour, belief systems, and opinions. We are divided. Our fear and intolerance can now be so easily manipulated. Are we being manipulated for our own good, or are we being manipulated for the good of the leaders we have chosen to follow?

What happens when we place in positions of power individuals who are prepared to manipulate us to help them forward their own self-interests? Are they really worried about us, or are they manipulating us to protect their own agendas? Won't they deceive us in some way to have us fight battles that only represent their own self-interests? You might bring up instances where we've gone to war to stop atrocities, but why the fuck are those atrocities happening in the first place? Do we want them to continue? Is it working for us?

We somehow become willing to kill. And for what? We might be terrified of losing something that might not be in actual jeopardy. If we are actually in danger of losing anything, isn't it because other people's fears and intolerances have been manipulated by the people they follow? What if we were simply to choose not to follow them any longer? We have the power to do that, regardless of what we have been led to believe.

Our militaries have been structured to maintain a chain of command. What if our soldiers don't agree with their orders? Is that tolerated? Absolutely not. It is all about control. And what we are forgetting as soldiers is that we can simply stop. We actually have all of the power in these situations, but we have been manipulated to believe that we don't. If we are even to start thinking about not following orders, we are reprimanded immediately.

What happens next is mystifying. We will deplete our world of precious resources in order to create more advanced technology and weaponry, whose sole purpose will be to kill before being killed. We stock supplies like food (or toilet paper) for fear that we might run out of these things while we are fighting. We then nurture an argument. Escalation is inevitable. Our fear and our intolerance become frenzied, and we eventually find ourselves capable of taking lives.

Then we set out to destroy one another. We take lives, we attempt to conquer the technologies of our foes, and we destroy all of those stockpiles of food and material. We send all of our own precious resources to the bottom of the sea, or we turn them to dust. Isn't this a colossal waste of everything? All we have accomplished is the loss of those things that are irreplaceable. We lose resources, we lose our sanity, we lose our own lives, and we lose our humanity. We will completely destroy one another, and turn our planet into something unrecognizable. And for what?

We seem to be naturally oblivious to the pain and suffering that are right around the corner. Just talking about war conjures unimaginable imagery of grief, pain, loss, and fear. Is that seriously what we have resigned ourselves to accept? The inevitability of pain and suffering? What the fuck is wrong with us?

How can we avoid war you ask? Tolerance. Stop being manipulated. Are we actually going to war to defend our way of life, or is our fear being manipulated? Aren't we actually being manipulated to go to war to force the ideologies of our leaders on other communities? If we can't make a unified decision, right now, to adopt more tolerant perspectives on a world-wide scale, we are setting our children up to fight wars based on nothing more than our own fears and our own intolerances. They will fight them because we were incapable of coming together as human beings. Our differences in religious beliefs or political ideologies, or our incalculable greed have let us justify sending our current and future generations to fight for our lack of tolerance. We are doing it right now. Everywhere. The scale might differ greatly, but the idea is the same. Do you not see people all over the world killing one another in this moment? Are we not on the brink of war in all kinds of political theatres? Most of us are turning a blind eye. What if the soldiers who are doing the fighting start to question how they are being manipulated? What if we all just stop?

Take a moment and have a look at social media. If you are able, tune into your local or international news mediums. Are you not privy to conflict on any scale? Is there not belligerent intolerance everywhere? People are driving us crazy. Instead of garnering amusement from watching videos of these people's seemingly insane behaviour, should we not pay more attention to what exactly is driving these people to these levels of insanity? Shouldn't we be concerned about humanity?

Most of us watch this shit, have a laugh (or a cry, for that matter), and go about our daily lives. Our blood boils momentarily, but then our emotions dissipate into a general indifference. We try to ignore the bullshit by telling ourselves that there isn't anything we can do about it. We can. It is absolutely within our power. We can strive toward a more tolerant way of thinking. We can pass that way of thinking onto our children, and they can pass it on to their children. We are capable of change.

How are we going to do that? Discussion. Open, tolerant discussion. We can start doing it right now. What would you like to see change? If it's conflict and war that you crave, then we are headed in the right direction! If you'd like to explore any means by which we might strive toward peaceful coexistence, or if you'd like for your kids to have a future that doesn't involve sacrifice, pain, fear, and suffering, then why don't we open our minds to this idea of tolerance on a world-wide scale?

What about our political, religious, or financial leaders that would prevent that discussion? Fuck them! They have no power over any of us if we choose to ask ourselves how we are being manipulated. They have no power over us if we all refuse to follow them or fight their battles for them any longer. Our manipulators need us to fight their wars for them. What if we were to all just stop following them? What if we were to all just stop fighting? There are too many of us; they can't silence us all.

If you believe that you are being manipulated by your elected or non-elected officials, all you have to do is set aside your fear and lay down your weapons. There is nothing they can do about it. The same weapons that you plan to use to destroy your foe will be the same weapons your advisory will use to destroy you. Like you, they are capable of inflicting maximum pain, destruction, and suffering upon you and your family.

Should we call for a rebellion? Maybe. We must be careful not to have it escalate into an armed one. That shouldn't be our desire at all. All we need is the willingness to put our collective guns on the ground. Isn't it interesting that the idea of laying down our armaments conjures up far more fear than it does any sense of relief? Is there not something intrinsically wrong with our thinking? Who do you think is responsible for making us feel that way?

Wouldn't it be amazing to explore what a world without war might look like? Should the idea not illicit some excitement in all of us? If our leaders promote war, why then are we allowing them to have any sort of power over us? If they desire to lead us into battle, we have the ability to just say no. What if we were to decide that we will no longer be manipulated? What if we simply choose not to sacrifice ourselves or our families in order to placate their own misguided fears or their corrupt aspirations?

Wouldn't you much rather be part of a discussion based in tolerance? Wouldn't you rather explore any and all avenues of peaceful resolution before subjecting your children to a world of pain and suffering? You might argue that the magical idea of peaceful resolution has been tried before. I would argue that it has never been sufficiently attempted with rigorous tolerance in mind, nor with the absence of fear.

We don't have to search very hard to find ourselves immersed in discussions about the apocalypse. Don't we all, in one way or another, have an imaginary picture of what the end of the world will look like? Isn't that screwed up? We play games, we watch movies, or we tell stories based on our ideas of what life will look like after the apocalypse. We are fascinated by "doomsday-preppers", but silently wonder if they are really as crazy as we make them out to be. We are actually resigned to the inevitability of world-wide chaos and destruction. Seriously? Shouldn't we be trying to avoid that eventuality at any cost?

Isn't it fascinating that the closer we get to our own death, the less concerned we seem to be about the state in which we will pass this planet on to the next generation? Why, then, have we chosen old men and women to be at the helms of our governments? Shouldn't we rather have a bunch of 12-year-olds directing us toward our future? They would do a much better job. There would be better ideas floating around. There certainly would be a lot more hugging.

What are you going to tell the next generation? "Sorry kids, your parents fucked up just a bit here. Best of luck." Can you think of a more astonishing thing to say? We are so much more concerned with our own selfishness and self-centeredness that we are demonstrating a reckless disregard for their future. "Sorry, kids, for setting you up to hate one another. Yup, we knew what the end result was going to be, but we did it anyway." What are you going to tell them when you send them off to war?

Why don't we imagine, instead, what the world might look like if the people we choose to put in positions of power are living by the principles we will shortly discuss?

Principled people are out there. Among all of us there are amazing, open-minded, spiritual individuals who are not driven by greed in the slightest. To them, the idea of war is a sickening proposition. Let's put them in charge!

These people exist in every community, every geographical setting, and every single demographic on the planet. What if we find a way to put these people at the helms of our governments world-wide? Wouldn't you be able to sleep better at night? Why don't we start moving in that direction? What if we were to start judging our potential leaders based on their ability to be tolerant over any other political ideology? We can do that right now. For these ideas to gain any traction, we must find a way to invite people from all over the world to join the conversation. How do you want to set out to accomplish this?

Religion Twisted

Can you think of a more heated topic than religion? We fight wars over this shit. We are prepared to kill one another for simply harbouring a different belief system with respect to what spirituality means to the individual. And what right do we have to do that? This isn't meant to be an attack on religion. It is only a plea for some tolerance.

We have incorporated into our religious structures this idea that we must disbelieve in other religions. The idea is flawed. Religious societies are often preying on our intolerance for other religious societies. Just open any history book and you will find all kinds of instances where wars have been fought over differences in religious belief systems. How are we to answer the questions of our children when they ask us why wars even exist? The only answer that I'm able to come up with is, "We fight wars, kids, for no other reason than we can't seem to come to any sort of agreement on anything to do with the spiritual. We are trying to teach you to be tolerant, but please do as we say, and not as we do."

Spirituality is a deeply personal experience, but challenge yourself to find a collection of people, anywhere on the planet, that haven't organized certain aspects of their society to adhere to a specific set of spiritual principles or ideologies. The ideologies are diverse. Even the ideology of atheism is bound by a belief in the "does not exist". So, the atheists among us actually have a structured belief system, too. Their belief systems are based on the disbelief in any kind of universal energy. They have a perspective of the spiritual without acknowledging the fact. They are spiritual by disassociation. Who can blame them? Haven't we all severely fucked up what spiritual principles and ideologies are supposed to be all about?

For the agnostics in the crowd, "I don't know" is serving you just fine. For the atheists among you, you have taken the stance that there is proof of the non-existence of any sort of spirituality. If these are serving you, wonderful. For those of you who have chosen to align your belief systems with a particular religion, superb.

Where we screw this whole thing up is when we adopt the belief that, "We are right, you are wrong". This is just a resurfacing of our own intolerance once again. And what happens? We all get our metaphorical shit in a knot, and we attack one another for nothing more than differences in our opinions on the spiritual.

What if we were to suppose that we are all correct in our belief systems? Can it not be argued that spirituality is an intrinsic human characteristic? Is it not all-inclusive and available to anyone who seeks it? Atheism is nothing more than a disbelief in that statement. Atheism is the conclusive denial of something that most of us will never fully understand. It is actually an expression of spirituality by disassociation.

If you are an atheist, is it because you find yourself reserved about signing up for any religion where the ideas are based on the spiritual philosophies that have been molded to suit that particular religious association? You don't have to sign up. Spirituality is within each and every one of us. If anyone tells you otherwise, they are lying to you. Nobody among us has actually met God. We don't know what "He" or "She" or "It" looks like. To claim that we do just isn't true.

We don't have to have any idea what this thing we choose to call God looks like, but doesn't it exist, nonetheless? Isn't spirituality something that none of us fully understands? Are we responsible for making the grass grow? All we need to know is that, if you simply add some water and sunlight, it is likely going to happen. Why do we feel like we need to explain everything all the time? What if we were to adopt the idea that we are connected with our spirits simply when we are feeling good? We don't have to describe our spirits, we don't have to understand them, and there is certainly no need to defend them. So why do we feel like we must?

A great number of you have already experienced this connection with spirit, in one form or another, regardless of what you believe in. Unfortunately, where we will now get this whole thing so very wrong is when we start believing that our connection with the spiritual is the direct result of a particular belief system. It isn't. We have connected with the spiritual simply because we have tried to do so with an open mind.

If you've experienced the connection, it is incredibly powerful and life-altering. The mistake that you will make is having the belief that you've connected with your own spirit solely in response to your own specific religious ideology. You have tapped into an unimaginable source of power, and therefore have proven to yourself that your ideology is correct. What you are failing to acknowledge is the fact that billions of people have tapped into this same sense of happiness and purpose that you have discovered, all while believing in something completely different than what you have attached your meaning to. There are people everywhere who are connecting with the spiritual, all the while having no idea at all about what it is that they are actually connecting to. We should be listening to them all.

Time and again, people are overcome with peace, love, joy, and a sense of fulness that they believe is uniquely available to them based on the religious ideologies that they've adopted. They think they've tapped into this power only because of their own belief system. With good intention, they want to share that experience with you. It isn't working. There is some built-in intolerance for any other belief systems here. Why are we letting our ideas on something that we can never fully understand divide us so completely?

What we are forgetting, and even will not tolerate, is that this spiritual connection is available to anyone, regardless of what religious practices (or lack thereof) they adhere to. To tap into spirituality, the only requirement is that you are human. All that any of it requires is open-mindedness and the willingness to believe. Do we actually want to believe that billions of people, who are all claiming to have experienced their own conceptions of God, are lying to us? If that were working, great. It isn't.

Spiritual experiences happen every day outside of any organized religious society. People become willing to believe in something, they decide to search for that something with an open mind, and their own spirits have revealed themselves. Therefore, couldn't we say that the potential for us to connect with the spiritual is available to anyone and everyone? You do not have to be special in any way. You are capable of connecting with a power that will bring you peace and happiness in your own life, regardless of what people would have you believe.

For peaceful coexistence, all that we have to do is to rid ourselves of this intolerance towards other people's conceptions of the spiritual. All we have to do is abandon our black and white ways of thinking.

None of you are wrong in any of your belief systems, and none of you are exactly right. People make spiritual connections every day. The only qualification to do so is the fact that you are human. Who are you to tell anybody that they are wrong? If you seek the freedom of religious expression, then shouldn't you allow for other forms of religious expression? To do otherwise defines you as nothing more than a hypocrite.

Must we then abandon any of our religious faiths? Absolutely not. If your spiritual belief system is working to give you purpose, serenity, happiness, direction, and satisfaction within your own life, who is to tell you that you are wrong? If you aren't hurting anyone, why should anyone ask that you change your belief system? Can we not all allow for the space for everyone to practice their own expressions of faith? Would we not be living in a world with far fewer arguments over our conceptions of the spiritual? Would we not regret any and every single war that we've ever fought to uphold our religious freedoms? Would we not be ashamed? Would we not be remorseful?

Prayer and meditation are of primary importance here. Pray to whatever you want to, as long as you believe that the entity receiving your prayers is infinitely more powerful than you. That's all it takes. Nothing more. Why not run the experiment? Every single human being has a spirit. None of our spirits are exactly the same. You will know when you are connected with your own spirit when you feel good about yourself. When you feel lost, empty, incomplete, intolerant, or bored, you are simply experiencing a disconnection from your spirit.

Your spirit is unique to you. Some people connect through prayer, meditation, or exercise. Others connect through reading or writing. Many people find artwork to be an expression of their spirit. A healthy lifestyle keeps many spirits happy. Some people find a connection with spirit through an honest interaction with other people. There are people who will tell you they find a spiritual connection whenever they are outdoors. Experiencing music or the arts encourages connection. We should believe in all of these things. It matters not how you go about connecting. The only thing that matters is that you do.

What fills your spirit will be unique. What works for you will not work for everybody. Wouldn't it be wonderful to tolerate however one chooses to connect with their spirits? Wouldn't many of our religious intolerances simply disappear? Our arguments will dissipate. Wouldn't we be more inclined to seek a common good?

If you are someone that cannot or will not accept that any other spiritual connection could exist beyond your own definition, ask yourself why that is. Wouldn't we be wiser to abandon our judgments? What makes you so right and everyone else so wrong? Could it be remotely possible that your intense connection with the spiritual has been exploited or manipulated into the belief that only you could be correct about these things? Why do you even need to be correct?

We also seem to adopt this idea that our spiritual leaders are uniquely more qualified than any of us in talking about spirituality. Aren't we all the same? Our religious leaders are very likely much more educated than we are in any particular doctrine, but does studying alone place these people higher on the spiritual totem pole than we should find ourselves? Anybody can study anything and become well versed in the doctrine. Why, then, do we allow them to claim importance over all of us? If they are the sons and daughters of God, aren't we all?

Spirituality is universal. There are plenty of spiritual people within all religious organizations. There are also many individuals within those religious organizations living lives that are wildly disconnected from any spiritual principles that I have ever learned about. Why do we continue to allow them to maintain their status within these organizations? Why do we follow them?

We seem to be oblivious about what is really going on. Whether you find yourself in alignment with this particular religious faith or that one, you should always be encouraged to connect with your own personal spirit. Why do we try so hard to align our belief systems with any kind of doctrine? We often follow people who can, if they are honest, only tell us that they aren't entirely sure about how this spirituality thing actually works. If they are trying to convince you that they alone possess that knowledge, they are full of shit.

In so many cases, the very religious leaders we have chosen to follow epitomize intolerance. If your spiritual leaders are promoting intolerance toward other religions, or if they would have you disrupt the spiritual practices of those who do not align with their own belief systems, why are you following them? Why are you paying their salaries and filling their coffers while they manipulate your own personal connection to the spiritual? They have convinced you that their way is the only way. It has to stop. We should be striving for more acceptance and tolerance as if our very lives depend on it. What if they actually do?

In other cases, we twist the message ourselves. Isn't history dotted with figures who were spiritually enlightened? Weren't they trying to help their fellow humans connect with the spiritual principles they had come to discover? Did they not all promote honesty, community, peace, and tolerance? Weren't all of these people trying to spread a message of hope? Haven't we so often twisted their message? Haven't we altered our ideas to misrepresent what spirituality is supposed to be all about? Would these historical figures not be disappointed in us? We will never know because they are all too often silenced.

Why don't we also challenge our own ideas on Heaven and Hell? What if Heaven and Hell aren't destinations? What if we are experiencing either Heaven or Hell right this minute? What if that was the message all along? If there is any truth to this, then you have the ability to experience Heaven or Hell from this moment forth. Wouldn't that be an idea worth exploring? If you are happy, are you not experiencing a sort of Heaven on Earth? If you are suffering, are you not already experiencing Hell? Where did this "destination" idea originate, anyway? What if we've got it all wrong? If you believe that Heaven and Hell exist, wouldn't it be easy to tolerate the opinion that they don't? If you're right, and indeed they do exist, how does the idea that someone disagrees with you affect you in any way?

If your life is providing you with, peace, happiness, and serenity, then your spirit is content. Shouldn't we all be supporting one another in every aspect of our spiritual journeys? If we are experiencing any form of Hell in our lives, shouldn't we be asking ourselves how we can help one another?

Spirituality is intensely personal. The possibilities for connection are limitless. However you want to connect with your own spirituality, there are amazing people among us who will show you the way. All it takes is an open mind and some practice.

Spirituality is the next "self-help" revolution. It is following in the footsteps of exercise, eating healthy, engaging in community, and spending time in nature. We have realized that prayer and meditation are of equal importance for us to feel good about ourselves. They are paramount to an experience of well-being. If we are to believe the billions, connecting with your spirit through prayer and meditation is an amazing experience. It gets us out of our own heads. It sets us up to seek out every other avenue by which we might achieve a similar feeling. Spirituality improves our mental health.

It is okay if you don't want to believe in the spiritual experience of "spirit". The idea here is that your spirit is within you whether you acknowledge it or not. Your spirit is happy whenever you are feeling good about yourself. If you are feeling bad, or if you are experiencing any sort of Hell in your life, you have simply been disconnected from your spirit. Reconnecting with your spirit will only serve to benefit you. Why disagree before you have honestly given it a try?

The Service Secret

The fastest and easiest way to connect with your own spirit, the most gratifying thing that you can do with your life, is to look for ways in which you might be able to help others. It allows us to get out of our own heads. In doing something for someone else, you will find yourself graced with the experience of true happiness. There will be no room for your own self-seeking. You will stop caring so much about yourself, and you will pay more attention to others. If there were a secret to life, this is it.

None of us are saints. We will often revert to self-centered thinking and behaviour, but whenever we do this for any length of time, we are missing out on something. Selfish pursuits never lead to true happiness. Not until we shift our thinking and ask ourselves how we might help our kids, our families, our communities, strangers, or even our planet, will we begin to experience anything resembling spiritual satisfaction. This will be so much easier to do if we can find a way to adopt some tolerance for our fellow humans!

It doesn't have to be anything monumental. Something as simple as a smile or a genuinely interested connection with another human being will suffice. If we are truly engaged with problems other than our own, there is no time to ruminate on what we consider to be wrong with our own lives. Try it. It works every single time.

Another secret to this phenomenon of service is that you must not tell anybody about your gestures of kindness. As soon as you tell someone, you've let go of any deeply resonating effects that are associated with the deed. You've robbed yourself of that spiritual energy. Keep it solely between you and whatever your conception of God, or spirit, might be. Your spirit knows what you've been up to. It will congratulate you with feelings of personal achievement and wholeness.

And what is going to happen if we all take on the mission of service? Can you imagine? What if we were to visualize a world full of people seeking to do nothing more than to be of service to one another? The wonderful dichotomy here is that we will all, in turn, feel better about ourselves. True happiness guaranteed.

Wouldn't that be a world we would be proud to pass on to our children? Get out there and help someone! If you honestly don't feel better about yourself, and if you honestly don't start to find some of that elusive happiness that some of us are claiming to experience, simply stop doing it. The only time you would want to get back is the time you just spent helping another person. Do you truly want to let a lack of interest in other people be the only barrier between you and your own true happiness?

Whoever you might be, you are capable of helping someone right now. Give them a call, share a hug, tell them they are important to you. It doesn't take much. Do it consistently for a while and check in with how you are feeling about yourself. You will feel better than you did yesterday. Honestly, what is it that you are afraid you might lose?

The COVID-19 pandemic has divided us more than we'd ever been divided before. Why not do what you can to brighten someone's day? What if you are even responsible for saving a life? You have no idea what the extent of your kindnesses might be. You have no idea how you might change a person's life today.

Martin Luther King was among the spiritually awake. He once said, "Life's most persistent and urgent question is, 'What are you doing for others?'"

We might find ourselves discouraged by the thought that this is going to require some work on our part. Isn't it true that our self-absorption is even more exhausting? Stop worrying about what everyone around you is doing. Only concern yourself with what you are up to. Stop pointing fingers. Why don't we all start to model some adult behaviour for our children?

Honesty

Rigorous honesty. It means you practice not telling lies. Isn't it strange that this takes practice? We are not just talking about the lies we weave into our own stories here. What about the lies we often tell ourselves? There is no faster way to disconnect from any form of spirituality than to tell a lie.

If you are a person who is quick to deceive for whatever reason, it is a habit that needs to be broken. It is both easy to do and extremely difficult. It is only difficult because what is about to be suggested here is uncomfortable. The next time you catch yourself lying, immediately correct yourself. You might say something like, "I'm really sorry, but I was full of shit just then. This is what really happened..." It is uncomfortable but effective. Your propensity to deceive will correct itself in no time. Openly correcting your own lies requires vulnerability and promotes tolerance from your fellows. You will undoubtedly discover the opportunity for some humor here. You will often have a laugh with whomever you are speaking. The conversation often evolves into a discussion about how you both do the same thing. You will find an immediate and honest connection. Give it a try.

The more difficult lies to identify are the lies that we tell ourselves. While our deceits to others will damage trust and connection with our fellow humans, the lies that we tell ourselves actually disconnect us from our own spirits.

So, what happens when we both lie to others and ourselves? Our spirits suffer and our self-esteem suffers. We are then further isolated by the utter inability to connect honestly with our fellow human beings. It is traumatic. We can crawl out of this self-imposed isolation by telling the truth in our stories and acknowledging the truth about ourselves. There are like-minded people everywhere. If we were to adopt the spiritual principle of honesty, we are bound to connect with them.

What is so elusive about self-honesty? It requires a lot of self-reflection. It is amazing how seldom we do this. How often have you been asked how you are doing, and you are quick to respond "fine" or "good"? Shouldn't there be a moment's pause before we answer? A moment of reflection? How are we actually doing? How are we actually feeling?

Whenever we take this moment of self-reflection, we will realize that our "fine" or "good" responses are often far from the mark. Typically, when we ask people how they are doing, are we truly invested in their response? Asking people how they are doing has become nothing more than a symbolic gesture. It shouldn't be. If we are doing the asking, we should absolutely be invested in the response.

What if we shift our perspective? What if we were to invest our energy into how someone is honestly doing? What if we assume that those people are truly invested in how we are doing? Wouldn't we be more inclined to practice any method of self-check-in available to us? We need to learn how to connect with our feelings and with others. We need to be taught how to do that effectively.

Wouldn't your interest in others actually grow if you assumed that they are also interested in you? What if the person asking you how you're doing is the person that is going to help you? Better yet, perhaps you are the only person today that will be able to help them. The possibilities for honest connection are limitless. Imagine what the world might look like if we were to practice both forms of honesty—being honest with others and with ourselves. We can start right now!

By learning how to check in with yourself, by learning how to properly share your thoughts and feelings, and by really paying attention to another's thoughts and feelings, you can start to communicate honestly. It takes practice, but it is ever so worth it. We are spiritual beings that require a sense of community to thrive. If the idea of a self-check-in with your own feelings is new to you, have a look at the appendix at the end of this book. Start trying to attach personal meaning to each one of these emotions. The purpose of this appendix is to help you identify with your feelings. If you can attach a word to how you are feeling, you are going to be able to learn how to recognize what you are feeling and when.

Shifting our behaviour to the practice of honesty, both with others as well as with ourselves, is going to allow us to experience this feeling of spirituality that we have been talking about. It will change your life. There is a reason you feel wrong when you lie. You have become disconnected from your own spirit. It is impossible to achieve any sort of unity with our fellow humans when we fail to figure out this honesty component to our spirituality.

Community

We have talked about how the lack of the spiritual principles of honesty, tolerance, and service are hurting us. There is one more important component to our problem. If the varying degrees of world-wide lockdown have proven anything to us, it is that we don't do well in isolation. Mental health problems have become an epidemic. We do not thrive when we are denied a sense of community. A sense of community is paramount to our well-being. It is a prerequisite to happiness.

Those of you who disagree have probably lost faith in the communities that are available for you. It can be difficult to become part of any community these days that isn't, in one way or another, fundamentally intolerant. It is equally difficult to become a part of any community that isn't structured around telling us how to think or how to behave. "Fall in line or you cannot be a part of our community" is often the message. So how do we end up feeling? Isolated and alone. Our spirits are suffering.

The only communities that we should be striving to become a part of are those that tolerate ideas and opinions that differ from the internal ideas and opinions of the community. Wouldn't you want to be a part of a community that is open to discussion? If your community's message is to have others come and join them, but members are required to start acting this way or behaving that way, why would anyone sign up for that? If we can't express any of our own experiences and ideas within the group, or better yet challenge some of the group's ideas, what are we even signing up for?

There are communities everywhere that, perhaps unintentionally, will not allow any difference of opinion. You might say that is the point. We have joined this community because we all think and feel this way. Do you really? Or have you been manipulated in some way to conform? When you think about it, do you completely believe in every single idea that your community represents? Do you believe it all on a spiritual level? If every person's connection with their own spirit is entirely unique, shouldn't we be allowed to bring our own ideas and experiences to the table? If any particular community would deny self-expression, do you really want to be a part of it?

It is incredibly simple to know if we are with the right people for us. All we have to do is listen to our intuition. We will instinctively know who we need to be around. Our spirits will guide us to the communities that will resonate with us. Don't you feel strange when you seek a connection with people who are disconnected from any form of spirituality? Doesn't it feel awkward when you try to connect with people who are intolerant or judgmental? Have you ever walked away from a conversation exhausted? There was a lack of a spiritual connection of any kind. You will intuitively know who you should be spending your time with. You have a built-in, spiritual barometer that will direct you to the people who will resonate with your ideas. All we have to do is listen to our spirits.

What if we promote more tolerant and all-inclusive communities throughout the world? Our spirits crave this sense of community. Look around the world and try to identify a place where we haven't formed communities surrounding every different ideological aspect of society. It's impossible. Forming community is instinctual. There is safety in numbers. Our survival depends on it. We aren't meant to be alone on this planet. Our spirits crave connection. We feel better around other people. It is a fundamental truth to our human experience. Tolerant communities promote tolerant communities. Wouldn't we be wise to promote more tolerant and less judgmental ones?

Pay attention to the communities around you. There are so many expressions of spirit. Listen to music, appreciate the arts, dance, play sports, take interest in the spiritual expressions of all human beings. Surround yourself with those people whose spirits will appreciate your own. Why don't we focus on forming communities around spiritual expression and principles?

Gangs, criminal organizations, political parties, or religious institutions tend to manipulate our primal necessity for community. We often won't agree with what they stand for, but we will become a part of the community regardless, because they fill this internal need that we humans have for company. They are often not spiritual at all. They might initially feel good to become a part of because our basic instincts for community have been met. They will never, however, completely satisfy our spirits if they refuse to tolerate our own individualism. It doesn't work if they seek to control us.

The only communities we should want to be a part of are the ones that satisfy our instinctual need for togetherness and that feel good to be a part of because of what they stand for. They are often the ones where spiritually connected people have come together to do something good. They promote individualism within the community, and they extend their kindnesses and tolerance to other communities, as well. It feels good to be a part of them because they enrich our spirits. It feels good to share ideas, and it feels good to help people. It doesn't feel good to be controlled. Promoting intolerance toward our fellow human beings will certainly never make us happy. The idea is flawed. It needs to stop.

Equality

Humans are instinctively pre-programmed to find any means by which to qualitatively divide ourselves. Why is that? Why must we systematically categorize ourselves into narrow descriptions of any particular group of people? We do it all the time, and it doesn't make any sense. Why are we incapable of just looking at ourselves as human beings? Would there not be far less suffering if we simply chose to do that? We fight wars over this shit, too.

We will actually murder one another because of differences in skin colour, culture, race, political or religious ideologies, gender, or even sexual orientation. We kill ourselves for nothing more than differences in opinions on how we should be living our lives. Are we fucking crazy?

The methods we employ to separate ourselves are mystifying. Upon any scrutiny, they make no sense whatsoever. Let us just take a look at skin colour. It is a fast and easy way to qualitatively describe how we are different. It promotes division. Not only is it insane, but it is also fundamentally wrong. Are "Black" people actually black? Nope. How about "white" people? When we put on white clothing is there no contrast between it and the colour of the skin? Absolutely there is. Are "red" folks red or "yellow" people yellow? Think about that for a moment. Every single one of us are, quite factually, occupying skins that are nothing more than different shades of brown. In the end, we are all actually just humans of similar colour.

So why do we define ourselves based on these arbitrary words that are bewilderingly incorrect? Is it because we have this built-in, seemingly instinctual habit of dividing ourselves? Perhaps there was a time when this served our collective purpose. Maybe we needed a method of distinguishing ourselves early in our evolution as a means of survival. Do we want to keep doing that? Is it working for us any longer? Do we seriously want to kill one another for occupying a skin that is nothing more than a shade of brown different from our own? Do we want to be killing one another for any of our other qualitative differences? It happens every day. What the fuck are we thinking?

If you combine our propensity to divide and our indescribable thirst for war, we will inevitably destroy one another until every single one of us looks exactly the same, believes in exactly the same things, and behaves in exactly the same manner. Is that seriously the direction we want to go?

Skin colour is only one example. We have innumerable descriptions of one another that seemingly serve no other purpose than to facilitate division among us. We also kill one another over differences in gender, sexual orientation, political opinions, religious ideologies, or even arguments over perspectives and opinions. And for what? Do we actually feel any better about ourselves? Does our fear subside? Do we feel any safer? I don't think so.

Nothing ever satisfies us. Instead, once we have successfully destroyed one community of people for not agreeing with us, we move onto the next community and start the discrimination process all over again. We need to recognize this as a fundamental fault within our own human nature. It takes a level of awareness to go about affecting any change. Wouldn't you like to see some change? How are we going to go about affecting the basics of human nature? Our problem is that doing so feels fundamentally impossible. If we are instinctually pre-programmed to find division amongst ourselves, and then we proceed to fight over it, we will be inclined to continue to look for that division, and we will proceed to kill one another because of it. We need to recognize this about ourselves. Awareness is the precursor to change!

Humans are actually nothing more than animals. We are predators. But are we making use of this human characteristic in any way that is working for us? Not at all. So, what are we going to do about it? We need something else towards which to focus our divisional energies. What if we were to suggest an alternative? What if we were to start by adopting this idea that we are all the same? Let's call ourselves "human" for a moment, or "Earthlings", if you will. That shouldn't require very much mental stretch-work at all. Let us shift our perspective to defining "humanity" as the global community that we are all a part of. Can't we all agree on that? What if we then place the highest importance on this idea of humanity? We would be inclined to protect it. We would be inclined to fight for its preservation, rather than continue fighting to destroy it.

If this propensity for division is instinctual, it will certainly take no small amount of tolerance and acceptance for us to change our behaviour. It will require a world-wide shift in perspective. We will have to forgive. Are we capable of any or all of this? Absolutely we are.

So how will we satisfy our desire for division? Where will we focus the energy of our own survival instincts? If division is in our very nature, we are going to require something upon which to re-focus our divisional instincts.

What if we were to imagine a threat to our global community coming from somewhere outside of our own solar system? We often do exactly that. There are a lot of movies that explore ideas surrounding a perceived external or "extra-terrestrial" threat. We are fascinated by them. And the overwhelming feeling behind each movie is that we must come together as a planet to overcome the threat. While you watch these films, isn't it a good feeling when the characters somehow manage to rally around a common purpose?

Why don't we just decide to assume that these external threats are not only real, but they are inevitable? It shouldn't take a gigantic mental commitment to imagine that we are not alone in the universe, should it? It is rather close-minded to say that these propositions are impossible. If we are honest, the best we should be able to bring ourselves to say is, "We don't know". We don't need to know. It doesn't matter if it is true or not. If we collectively decide to believe it to be true, we will have a target toward which we can focus that instinctual divisional energy. We will have a common goal that we can work toward as a community of humans. Protecting this planet becomes our focus. We could certainly stop killing one another.

Who gives a shit if we are never visited by a hostile alien civilization? If we simply assume that it is going to happen, wouldn't we have something that will divert our attention from how we are all different? If we can just agree that we are nothing more than Earthlings, could we not stop killing one another over our internal differences?

If you aren't fascinated by where this idea might lead us in the future, why not? And if there exists even the remotest possibility that this arbitrary philosophy was to never materialize, would our time have been wasted? We put immense value on our international militaries. We like to parade them as expressions of power. It is instinctual that we develop them as a means by which we can defend ourselves, should the need arise. Why not bring them all together with a common purpose? The arms contractors would be satisfied. Our fascination with more advanced weaponry would be satisfied. We just wouldn't be using any of it to kill one another. It is a goal worthy of our efforts.

The self-infliction of pain and suffering could stop today. What are your thoughts? Who among you wouldn't be interested in, at the very least, exploring the idea? Shouldn't we be insanely curious as to how, with a simple shift in our global perspective, we might go about averting war?

Financial Pyramid Schemes

Our financial systems are broken, making it impossible for us to come together as fellow humans. There exists an illusion that capitalism rewards hard work. But does it necessarily reward everyone who works hard? At the other end of the spectrum, we have this idea of communism. There is also an illusion that communism only exists to help the people it represents. Is that what we are seeing in the world today where countries are operating within a communist ideology? Are the people being helped or are they being oppressed?

I will say it again: whether you find yourself aligning with either of these political systems and their financial repercussions, the systems themselves are broken. They are corrupt. People are suffering, regardless of what ideas or systems on the political-financial spectrum they support. People are suffering within any of the constructs we have created to appropriate our distribution of wealth. Nothing seems fair for everyone. Perhaps it isn't even the systems themselves, but how we've become accustomed to corruption by our socio-political leaders. Don't we want to create a system that works for everyone on this planet?

Can we even explain to ourselves why we have become accustomed to a massive disparity of wealth between the richest and the poorest among us? How many of you are currently working in careers that you are passionate about? If not, what would you rather be doing? Why aren't you doing it? Could it be that we've put an astronomically twisted value on financial wealth? Is money truly the only thing we want to rely upon to make us happy? Wouldn't it be interesting if we were all encouraged to pursue careers that we are truly passionate about? What do you think the world might look like?

The way we've set these systems up, there are billionaires inhabiting the same planet as the starving. Are we to argue that the billionaires have worked much harder than the starving? Are we not deceiving ourselves here? How do you think it will go for you if you try to explain to a mother, on her miles-long march for fresh drinking water, that if she were only to work harder, she will have the ability to accomplish more in her life? Could you even tell her that with a straight face? More concerning is the fact that you might actually be aligning yourself with this belief without even realizing it. Our capitalist societies function on this idea. We are being manipulated on a colossal scale.

Are you going to seriously believe that the CEO of some company has made billions because they are smarter than you or because they worked harder than you ever did? We have set up our society in such a manner where we actually believe this makes some kind of sense. Why do we continue to support it? At the other end of the spectrum, we find the leaders of these supposedly socialist or communist countries also insanely wealthy. What the fuck is going on?

Why have we created a means by which these people can become so insanely wealthy? Are we not being manipulated once again? We are either made to believe that these people deserve it, or we have been manipulated to accept that this is just the way things are. And in all of this, there seems to be a need to convince us to spend our money on shit we don't need. They lead us to believe that we need these things to be happy. It's all a lie. The only people that are actually benefitting are the people at the heads of these systems. The rest of us are nothing more than unwitting participants. Our financial systems aren't working. They are failing over 90% of the people on our planet.

Many of the wealthiest people in society haven't necessarily risen to their positions of power solely of their own accord. They are often born into their positions, or they had help in achieving them. Think about our so called "Royal Families". Why have we accepted their dominance over us? These people are nothing more than human beings, and often not even very good examples of humanity. For some reason, we continue to worship them. We continue to make them rich beyond explanation. They are no different than you, me, or anyone else for that matter. But we are somehow led to believe that they are. What the fuck are we doing, people?

Many of our wealthiest citizens have attained that status at the expense of those of us who work for them, or they've attained their status at the expense of the planet. The groundwork for keeping these systems running was put into place a long time ago. Is it even possible for most of us to gain access to these systems? Something needs to change.

We have allowed for a metaphorical "pyramid scheme" to develop with respect to the division of wealth throughout our global societies. The rich stay rich, while it is almost impossible for any of us to even attempt to join them. The tiers of these pyramids represent the division of wealth within whatever organization we want to examine. The tiers themselves are occupied by individuals who are satisfied with the financial compensation they are given for their work. The closer anyone finds themselves to the top of these pyramids, the better the compensation. They will experience inexplicable levels of wealth the higher they manage to climb within the pyramid's system. They are placated.

When you observe these systems, do you necessarily find incrementally more intelligent or hard-working people at the higher tiers of compensation? No. So what is actually happening? We have created a structure of wealth that is fundamentally broken. It doesn't seem to work for the majority of the population. It is almost impossible for anyone to insert themselves into these systems. Our ability to become a part of the system is most often predetermined.

People are born into these systems, or they are brought into them through powerful connections. You might disagree. If so, can you explain how someone born into a Third World country, regardless of their intelligence or propensity for hard work, is going to find any kind of foothold in any of these exclusive financial systems that we have created in our world?

Not only does it take money to attain an education but, upon completion of that education, your potential for employment is often based on where you live or who you know. Our financial systems are structured to keep the fortunate fortunate. They spend little time worrying about the rest of society. The people at the top of these pyramids have often found something about society to exploit. It is usually something to which we've assigned an arbitrary level of value. The entertainment industry and the sports industry are just a few examples of how these systems thrive. They have found a way to manipulate us into paying exorbitant amounts of money to support them, and they will do anything to maintain the system's structure. It is fine when the system is working for all of us, but we are often elevating people to ridiculous levels of wealth—people who have no business whatsoever being in these positions.

Most of these systems are operated by intelligent individuals who amass vast sums of money exploiting the talents of other people. It works because they've compensated their employees far above society's financial norms. The employees make millions of dollars, so they are happy and content to carry on. They are comfortable. We are manipulated to believe that we have to buy what they are selling in order to be content with life. Aren't these just different methods of controlling our behaviour?

For the heads of these financial organizations to maintain such a disproportional balance of wealth, they must convince you and I that the system is working. Enter the media, which is controlled by who? You guessed it! The media is controlled by the rich, who in turn distort the information to satisfy their personal interests. All forms of information flow are directly controlled by the people who oversee the operation of these systems. They are the people who are paying for the different forms of information distribution. Is it hard to believe that they might manipulate every aspect of information that they are feeding us?

If you were to place money above all else, wouldn't you do anything and everything in your power to make sure that things stay exactly the way they are? Of course. Wake the fuck up, people. It's happening every day in every corner of the world. The rich get richer at our expense, and we don't ever seem to do anything about it. We acknowledge corruption, and then we proceed to ignore it. We don't care if these people are assholes. Instead, we are led to believe that they deserve their position of wealth.

Why do we support extravagant salaries and wildly comfortable pension plans when we don't even support how these people have made, or continue to spend, their fortunes? In the case of politicians, is it even possible to vote anybody into these positions of power and extreme wealth that aren't already somehow a part of the system? The people we find ourselves able to vote for are generally wealthy, famous, or already well-connected. They can afford the media exposure necessary to attain or maintain power. Are we not wide-the-fuck-asleep?

Take a look at some of society's other metaphorical pyramid schemes. At the top we have owners, politicians, the religious elite, or CEOs. They are ridiculously wealthy, and they want nothing more than to stay in power. They have a pyramid of people underneath them who are the ones responsible for the successes of the organization. They recognize that without the people working for them the system will collapse. They will do anything and everything to protect the scheme.

Do we not see them endlessly labouring over avoiding having any of their employees piss us off in any way? As soon as we are upset, we refuse to support the system any longer. The owners and officials know this, so they protect their schemes by all means necessary. They are afraid of us. Rightfully so. They know full well that without us, these systems simply won't survive.

Watch a sporting interview. Do you think athletes of any particular league talk about how they honestly feel? These interviews are scripted. They aren't even interesting. The athletes sound like robots. The owners have provided coaching on how to respond to questions from the media. It is called "media-training". It is nothing more than a form of control. Any time an athlete speaks from the heart, they are reprimanded. The bigger the star, the more the owners will tolerate. For the average athlete, speaking in a manner that goes against the message the owners want us to believe seals their fate. Are the professional athletes among you not tired of this shit? It is you who are providing the product.

If you're a sports fan, it won't take you long to think of an example where an athlete has been blacklisted for a particular view that the ownership thinks might rock the boat. If these owners think that what these athletes have said or done will jeopardize the system in any way, they get rid of them as quickly as possible. It doesn't matter that they are good at what they do. The possibility that they might piss off the general public, and therefore risk a boycott of the system, is much too great for the ownership to risk keeping these people around.

The bigger the star, the more chances they will get. But in the end, if the ownership cannot bring them around to toe the party line, they will quickly cut ties with their employees. They are beyond intelligent. What they are doing is using our own intolerance against us. It makes us feel like we have a say in how the system is operating when, in actuality, we don't believe that we have any control over the system at all. We do. We have all the power. We just need to wake the fuck up.

What if we extrapolate this idea of pyramid schemes to every other financial or political system out there? Can you think of an example where an actor can no longer find any meaningful work? Absolutely. What about employees who are perceived to have crossed the line, although their opinions and behaviours have nothing to do with their employment situation whatsoever? Gone. What about people who demand change within their governmental systems? Silenced. Governments operate this way, our militaries operate this way, corporations operate this way, even our religious institutions operate this way.

Does the leadership really have a fundamental problem with what has been said or what has been done? Not necessarily. These "rebels" are fired from their positions, removed from society, simply to protect the people at the top. The people at the peaks of these pyramids want the money to continue to roll in. Those of us working in the lower tiers of their pyramid schemes are forever replaceable.

Why should we shine light on this behaviour? It is because we are buying into systems that in no way represent our collective ideologies. Even the individuals working within the systems have been conditioned. We are buying into nothing more than a facade. The people within the system are often oblivious, having been manipulated to conform. If you find yourself on the inside of one of these systems, are you content with your role in the organization? Are you able to have your ideas heard? Are you happy with the compensation you are granted for your hard work? If you aren't, could it be that you are just a component within a system whose function it is to make someone else wealthy or happy?

The only thing that matters to our puppet masters is that the structure of the pyramid schemes remains in place. Status quo. Are we going to continue to be okay with that? If you find yourself inside the system you might be, for you are comfortable or you are safe. But do you really have the freedom of expression? And what about the rest of you? What if you are unable to gain access to any of these systems whatsoever? Do you have access to post-secondary education? Or even primary education for that matter? Are you capable of becoming qualified for the career that interests you?

What should be concerning to all of us is, what is wrong with this picture? Imagine the possibility that there might be someone out there who has the intelligence to cure cancer. What if they will never do so, for no other reason than the lack of access to the associated systems that would help to develop their skillset? Wouldn't that be the tragedy of tragedies? We are missing out. Even more concerning is that we are allowing ourselves to be led, either politically, financially, or spiritually, by people who honestly don't really give a shit about any of us at all. They are using us.

What if we were to completely restructure society? What if we elect leaders who actually represent our own values? We don't need them to represent our opinions or our financial aspirations. What we should want them to be doing is representing the spiritual principles we have been talking about.

What if we make it our intention to allow every single human being on the planet to have access to the resources they need? Even if those resources are provided at the most basic levels, shouldn't we all have access to decent food, clean water, shelter, and education? We are absolutely capable of doing that. This is where a platform for international discussion based on tolerance and equality would be invaluable.

We have allowed those lucky enough to be at the pinnacles of these systems to have so much power and wealth that they aren't even sure what to do with it all. We don't need to make it our goal to take away any of their wealth or their power. Instead, why don't we challenge them on what they are doing with that wealth and that power? We have the right to do that. After all, isn't it our contributions that are keeping these systems running in the first place? If they aren't using their wealth and power for the betterment of the people working for them, why the fuck are we following them in the first place? Sure, there are philanthropists among the insanely wealthy who do use much of their money to help their fellow humans. But it certainly isn't universal. And couldn't even the philanthropists among them help even more?

Unfortunately, what do we most often see the wealthiest among us doing with their money? They own mansions that accommodate far beyond their basic necessities. They own more than one mansion. How many of these properties remain unoccupied most of the time? Why are they okay with all of these unoccupied properties and extravagances while there are starving and homeless people all around them? We never seem to challenge them, or we do, but they have the money to shut us up.

Why do the wealthiest people collect expensive things they don't even use? Is it because of boredom? They collect cars they never drive, countless purses, shoes and clothes that sit in closets, so much jewelry they couldn't possibly wear it all simultaneously, boats that they rarely sail, properties that they rarely visit, immeasurably valuable things that they hardly ever even bother to look at. Aren't these things all, at their core, nothing more than representational displays of power? They honestly are just examples of endless wasted dollars.

There are billionaires among us who are concerning themselves with space exploration. What the fuck for?

Shouldn't we be trying to get our collective, earthly shit together before taking our show on the road?

Significant portions of these fortunes could be better spent helping someone in need. Wouldn't you rather see them spending their money on the betterment of the planet, whatever that looks like to you? Why don't we challenge them to do exactly that? What if we were to stop supporting them in those cases where we disagree with how they go about diverting their power or their wealth? It is craziness.

The richest 10% of adults in the world are responsible for roughly 90% of global household wealth, give or take a few percent. What is even more disturbing is that the bottom half of the world's population collectively accounts for only about 1% of the combined household wealth on our planet. Is this sustainable? It takes no small effort on the part of the richest people in society to maintain the facade. Don't you think that at some point in the near future people will eventually have had enough of this bullshit? There is a revolution coming. Wouldn't you rather it be a peaceful one?

We often wonder why our crime rates are so high. Wouldn't you, if you were born into a situation where you had no access to education or meaningful employment, make use of anything and everything at your disposal to provide for your families? I know I would. We need to change our perspective on crime, too. If we could get everyone access to education and meaningful employment, we can surely expect our crime statistics to plummet.

We need to challenge our ideologies here. The wealthiest among us should revisit the discussions we've had on spirituality, honesty, service, and community. There is far greater happiness available to us all should we choose to seek it. Everyone will benefit. Everyone.

We should not necessarily judge the wealthiest or most powerful among us without scrutiny. Maybe some actually deserve to be rich. Instead, we should be paying attention to how these people set about making use of their positions of power and wealth. Do they help people, or have we made them rich and famous for no reason whatsoever? What if we were to start directing some difficult questions toward society's wealthiest individuals? What if we start to question these people on what exactly they are spending their money on and why? Do we want to keep living like this? What if we were to come together and explore alternatives that would much better care for every human being who calls this planet home?

Environment

How do you think we are doing taking care of our environment? How would you grade our efforts? We don't seem to have any unified perspective on what is actually best for this planet of ours. We are headed in the wrong direction. We have become incredibly wasteful. We throw out food in the Western part of the world, while people in other parts of the world starve. In war, we exploit our own non-renewable resources, only to blow them all up again. We are over-reliant on fossil fuels. This stuff doesn't replenish itself. We are currently pumping a shit ton of CO_2 into our atmosphere, all the while cutting down the trees that are required to filter the stuff. There is some irony here, and not of the humorous type. When it comes to our own environmental future, geniuses we are not.

We are currently affecting our own environment at our own peril. Weather patterns are shifting, we are destroying our oceans, there are daily extinctions in our animal kingdoms, we are losing our biodiversity at an alarming rate, and we raze forests to make room for food. We are seemingly oblivious to the fact that we need the oxygen that those forests provide us to even sustain life.

We, with all of our intelligence and technology, have failed to discover a means by which we can sustainably feed our global population. Or worse, we know exactly how to go about doing it, but for unexplainable reasons we are failing to do so. Our mindless striving for wealth and power is jeopardizing our own security. Our future is what is at stake here. We are oblivious.

Think about that for a moment. We have set up our society to worship wealth above all else. There are no boundaries to the environmental burdens that we will impose on our own planet, as long as there is money to be made. Are we insane? We must not give a shit about future generations at all. It is almost as though we have resigned ourselves to all kinds of environmental disaster, so we will spend our money and have as much fun as we can with the time that we have left. Self-absorbed would be an understatement. Self-centered assholes would be a better description of how we are behaving. As a matter of fact, self-centeredness is at the heart of almost all our problems.

Those who disagree, either don't believe in science or are afraid of what change might look like to their bank accounts. Mother Nature is screaming at us. The scientists are screaming at us. Some of us are starting to listen, but whether or not we are listening often depends on our geography, political situation, or financial position. There seems to be a general shift in our environmental ideologies, but it is happening far too slowly. We set future goals only to put our problems off until tomorrow. Isn't that human nature? It isn't going to work. We can't rely on our kids to fix things. There will be nothing left to fix. We need to change things now.

We need to look around. Every year, there are more and more fires around the world, extreme storms, polar melting, massive floods, changes in weather patterns, declining forestation and biodiversity, oceans on the brink of collapse, declining biomass, pollution, famine, war, chaos, disaster, disease. These things are not opinions. They are facts.

It is impossible to say what those who believe the environment is steadily improving are basing that opinion on. Where is the evidence? Might these people have their metaphorical heads in the sand? Perhaps they think they are incapable of changing anything, so they have resigned to hope for the best. Has ignoring a single problem in life ever worked? Do we really think that our planet is going to survive on hope alone?

The environmentalists among us already know what we are talking about. Even governments have begun to shift. They are slowly working toward change. Why so slowly? They know the quiet majority demands a change in perspective, but our governments have been put in power by the wealthy. They have been put in power, and are therefore responsible to the people who have made their millions at the expense of our planet.

These people aren't ready for radical change. Not if it would affect their financial well-being. What if we simply stop accepting anything other than immediate and radical change with respect to every single environmental challenge that we face? We could pull a metaphorical emergency brake here. That's exactly what needs to happen if we actually have any interest in diverting global environmental catastrophe. It is what needs to happen if we want to save this planet of ours. Can we not convince anyone who thinks otherwise that the preservation of our planet is far more important to our collective futures than fat, precious bank accounts?

Addiction

We need to talk about addiction because it is the silent plague of our time. It is killing our spirits and it is crushing our dreams. Addiction changes us from givers in life to takers from life. It robs us of our ability to do good in the world. It is distracting us, and it is killing us.

Addiction to anything is nothing more than an escape attempt. Our escape attempts work for a while, but eventually, by addiction's definition, they create problems in our lives. What are we trying to escape? Aren't we trying to escape our own realities and traumas? What is so wrong with our reality that we are seeking escape from it? We are a traumatized lot. Trauma reaches out to us from our past, it can be something we are currently experiencing, or we can experience trauma when we worry about our future. Whatever the trauma might be, it is unique to the individual experiencing it.

Traumas cannot, therefore, be compared. They are unique to the individual, and each person experiences trauma in their own way. One person's trauma, while seemingly insignificant to others, might impact them much more profoundly than one might expect. All we can do is try to relate with the traumatized. We need more empathy. People who have been traumatized in similar ways will find it easier to relate to one another. People everywhere are traumatized. Why wouldn't they want to escape the associated feelings? Welcome addiction.

What enters your mind when you hear the word "addict"? Do you picture a homeless, disheveled, dirty individual injecting substances into his or her own body? What if we use the word "alcoholic"? Do you picture a sad individual stumbling down the street, or someone abusing his or her own partner in fits of rage? For sure these examples are out there, but they are only single representations of what addiction can look like. More and more families are experiencing substance addiction on a personal level. More of us are becoming familiar with addiction and realizing that it can happen to anyone. Addiction does not discriminate.

What about the more subtle manifestations of addiction? Representations of addiction that we might not even be aware of. The list is extensive. The Merriam-Webster dictionary defines addiction as, "compulsive, chronic, physiological need for a habit-forming substance, behaviour, or activity having harmful physical, psychological, or social symptoms..." You see, people can be addicted to anything.

Drug addictions are the most commonly recognizable; however, people are finding escape through a whole host of addictive substances, behaviours, and activities. Exercise, sex, food, religion, cigarettes, caffeine, power, wealth, television, gaming, cellphones, social media, diets, pornography, shopping, control, gambling, co-dependency, adrenaline, the Internet, fear, isolation, body image, or even our methods of connectivity (dating, belonging, etc.) are only some of addiction's possible manifestations. When that substance, behaviour, or activity becomes harmful, but the person can't or won't stop despite knowledge of continued harm, that is addiction.

How many of us would not tolerate addictive behaviour in others, but engage in behaviours that align with another example of addiction's manifestations? Probably more than a few of us. We call this hypocrisy. Be honest, for we can't affect change without a little self-awareness. If you are using any substance, behaviour, or activity and it is causing you harm in any way, then you have an addiction. If you think you might have a problem with addiction in any of its manifestations, are you likely to continue to look down upon the homeless with the same amount of judgment? Probably not. Addiction is addiction.

All addiction originates from this underlying yearning for a means of escape. An escape from what? We are attempting to escape the traumas of our pasts, the traumas of the present, or the traumas caused by ruminating about our future. We are experiencing unwanted feelings, and we will escape them however we can. We crave distraction. Or we will use substances in search of a connection to something. Many substances, behaviours, or activities create a false sense of connection to whatever we feel like we are missing out on. Are you overwhelmed by a feeling of emptiness and isolation? Do you feel like you are missing out on a sense of belonging? Is your spirit craving something? For a while, our addictions will satisfy all of these feelings. We wouldn't continue to indulge in our addictions if they weren't working for us.

Unfortunately, over time, our addictions become substitutes for the connections we could otherwise make to our own spirituality on our own. They no longer sufficiently treat our traumas. Addiction eventually serves to only make the experience of our traumas even worse. What happens is that we become disconnected from our spirits over time. The substances, behaviours, or activities become less effective. They begin to cause more harm than they ever did before. We need more to get the same level of relief. Eventually, they stop working altogether. In many cases, they are even killing us.

The only way to beat addiction is to find a way to connect with our spirits. The only way to beat addiction is to find alternative means by which we can deal with our traumas. If we want to derail our addictions, our spirits are the only things that will fill the voids that have been vacated by the absence of our substances, behaviours, or activities of choice. Almost all the recovery programs out there find their foundations in this simple principle.

You might say, "How can my phone be an addiction? How can social media be an addiction? Sex? Exercise?" If any of these things are causing any kind of difficulty in your life, then by definition they are manifestations of an addiction. One addiction cannot be compared to another. One person's addiction to a particular substance, activity, or behaviour is often equally destructive when compared to one who is addicted to an entirely different substance, behaviour, or activity.

Do you sacrifice time spent with family and friends to sit at home and spend endless amounts of time on your gaming system? Can you only feel good about yourself when you are exercising? Are you irritable and discontented when you have misplaced your phone? When you experience anxiety, is it only placated by food? Are you obsessed with your body image, but you are never really happy, regardless of what you look like?

These are all examples of how addiction manifests itself. All these things become nothing more than substitutes for spiritual connectivity.

Why do we find it so hard to recover? Consider that, with the knowledge that we will need to find a connection with our spirit to recover from addiction, aren't we inclined to believe that our ships are already lost? We certainly aren't buying some of the interpretations of spirituality that our religious institutions are trying to sell us. What if we don't have to? What if we can form our own conceptions of the spiritual?

The religious people among us often quickly find an escape from addiction. This is only true if they practice the spiritual principles that are laid out for them within any particular religious organization. When they use their religion to access their spirituality, they are generally successful. When they don't make this connection, religion alone will not save them from their suffering.

It is often harder for the rest of us because we have come to believe that if we can't accept someone else's conception of God, we are quite doomed. There are millions of people who do, however, experience a spiritual awakening outside of any religious affiliation. There is hope for all of us.

If spirituality is the solution to addiction, and if spirituality is all-inclusive, every single one of us can experience recovery no matter what we believe in. It is only when we are led to believe that we are doing it wrong that we fail. So, if we can all adopt a mindset of tolerance for whatever form of spirituality people believe in, we would become better able to help one another on our individual roads to recovery.

Should we abandon all these addictive substances, behaviours, or activities? Quite the opposite, as a matter of fact. Are we going to ban cellphones? Do we want another era of prohibition? Probably not. What if we were to advocate for the legalization, and therefore the regulation, of all forms of addictive substances? Many of them have already been legalized, depending on where we live.

Is it difficult to believe that anyone wanting to find an escape, right now, could leave the house and be high in less than an hour? On anything. Are we ever going to stop people who want to use their substances of choice? If they want to use, they will find a way. We've tried to stop it everywhere, and we have failed miserably. What we need to do instead is take away the addict's reasons for using in the first place.

Legalization would simply take the money away from the criminals. Perhaps we could take all that money and put it to better use. Our war on drugs doesn't work. We have proven it over and over. Criminals are rich, and our loved ones are still suffering. They are still dying. The war on drugs is nothing more than a facade that we have been led to believe will work one day. It's bullshit.

What we also get wrong here is this idea that we must treat only the symptoms of addiction. On the contrary, what we have to do is to start treating the actual problem. We need to start treating our collective traumas. All our mental health is suffering. We don't like what we are experiencing, and we will do anything to escape our feelings. We will come to believe that spirituality is the solution. We must.

What if we pour immense resources into helping people connect with their spirituality? What if we devote massive amounts of money trying to understand how we can go about treating our individual traumas? Wouldn't we be directly affecting our necessity for escape? Wouldn't there be measurable, world-wide benefits to our mental health? Doesn't that sound like something worth striving toward?

Are you afraid of being denied your means of escape? Don't panic. If your substance of choice were to be legalized, you would be free to use to your heart's content. You are using them now anyway. Nothing would change for you, other than how the money used to purchase your substances of choice will be repurposed. Your money would simply no longer be contributing to the sustainment of criminal empires and organizations.

There is nothing wrong with anything in moderation. If your substance, activity, or behaviour isn't causing problems in your life then by definition it isn't an addiction. We just need to recognize that whatever we are currently using or doing to fill that spiritual void isn't working for us. It is either momentarily allowing you to feel like you are spiritually connected, or it momentarily takes away the negative feelings associated with your trauma. It isn't sustainable.

Instead, wouldn't you rather have access to the support you need to treat your trauma? If spirituality is the answer, wouldn't you like some help with discovering your own spirituality? What if we advocate for more properly trained mental health professionals and more spiritual teachers? What if more treatment centers begin to function from the perspective of treating our traumas, instead of attempting to teach us how to simply stop using?

If we are to win the battle of addiction, it will never be the result of a war on anything. We need to instead develop a clearer understanding of what addiction actually is. Addiction isn't something that can be treated solely from a medical perspective. There is an undeniable spiritual component to addiction.

We have discussed how the spiritual principles of honesty, service, and community might successfully treat our spiritual condition. There are innumerable 12-Step programs world-wide that successfully employ these principles to help people recover from all manifestations of addiction. None of this is new. You should be asking yourself how making use of these principles might help you in your own recovery.

Action

There have been people throughout history that have tried to promote some of these ideas. There have been spiritually enlightened people who have tried to spread these messages. What typically happens to them? They are removed from society by the powers that be. They are silenced.

Right now, in some countries, if people are challenging the ideas of their governments, they are being removed from the eyes of the public. Governments are afraid of anyone who might challenge their corruption. They have always been afraid of those people. They know that, if our ideas were to gain any traction, a revolution is inevitable. They are afraid and they would have us silenced. It's happening everywhere. What if there are simply too many of us to silence?

So where do we go from here? Where do you want to go? We need a peaceful revolution. A movement whose sole focus is the betterment of the planet. We need direction, and we need a tolerant platform for our discussions. We should no longer vote for or continue to support anyone in a position of power who does not have the condition of our planet as the primary focus of their leadership. It should be of paramount concern. It must be.

We need to start feeling better about ourselves. We need to help ourselves, and then we need to set out to help everyone around us. Our spirits need to be re-energized. We need to start believing that we can change anything that we make the focus of our collective energies. Whether we believe we can or we believe we can't, we are absolutely right.

If they are intolerant or if they are more concerned about their own well-being that the well-being of humanity, our religious leaders, our politicians, the media, the rich, the famous, the powerful, and the connected must be denied the power to manipulate. If you suspect that you are being distracted or manipulated, if you get the sense that your leaders stand for anything other than the healing of our planet, or if they illustrate to you an utter disregard or intolerance toward any individual that calls this planet "home", why don't you simply refuse to stand behind any of them any longer? It's that simple.

We should demand nothing more than rigorous honesty and transparency from our elected political and religious officials. After all, we have chosen them to lead us. If we are to call them public servants, they should be nothing more than servants to the public. Honesty and transparency must come with the job. But is this what we are seeing today? Absolutely not. If we continue to allow them to manipulate us, we are all in some serious trouble. We will see one another from across the next battlefields.

If you were to ask yourself whether you believe that you have ever been lied to or manipulated by your government or your religious leaders, what would your answer be? Most of us would agree that we have been. Why don't we put a stop to it? Demand that your chosen officials show you exactly where every single tax dollar goes. Better yet, question how they go about spending your money even on a personal level. Demand that they show you what they've been up to behind closed doors. No more secrets.

We are paying their salaries. We should be demanding radical transparency. If our elected officials are using our money to further their own personal financial gain, are you going to continue to accept that? Could we suggest that, if the leaders we chose to follow can afford all these properties or extravagances, we might be paying them far too much? Do we even want people who prioritize extravagance over democracy leading us to our collective futures? Corruption needs to stop.

If we continue to allow this shit to happen, we are attracting the wrong kinds of people to these positions of leadership. We are attracting people whose primary purpose for seeking out these positions of power is the accumulation of wealth. Do they really care about what we would hold important? Not likely.

Instead, what we are seeing is that these people will do anything and they will say anything to appease the majority of the population. They often don't even stick to their original promises. They will lie to us because they know that we will forgive their lies. Sure, they may be attempting to appease as many of us as possible, but it is far more important to them that they keep the wealthy happy. It is the wealthy that have helped them achieve their positions of power in the first place. They are responsible to the wealthiest among us. So, the systems will never change unless we change them.

Wouldn't you rather have any of these leadership positions occupied by people with different agendas? Wouldn't you rather see people in power who aren't concerned about material wealth at all? Wouldn't those types of people lean toward agendas that are much more important to the planet? Sure, they would. And these people are everywhere.

When it comes to any of these discussions, trust your spirits. They have an amazing, vastly intelligent, and curious nature about them. They are intuitive, and they speak to you often. We call this our "gut-feeling". All that your spirits want for you is peace, love, serenity, safety, and happiness. We must learn to listen.

Any of us can promote our movement. It is only important to become a part of it. It will work if there is no striving for wealth or power amongst any of us. It is why this book has been written anonymously. We will be successful if we manage to find a way to come together. We need to start with discussion. We will find infinite power in the sharing of our ideas. We will find infinite power in knowledge and understanding. We need to let go of our fear and replace it with tolerance. We can do this. Doubt prior to attempt is destroying our dreams.

Your ideas and suggestions are what will determine our direction. It is you who will shape the future of our movement. Please don't hold onto this book. Use the ideas contained here as a motivation for change, and then pass it on. These ideas are not owned by anyone. None of them are original. Wonder about how you might make use of them to help yourself and how you might use these perspectives and principles to help one another.

If you haven't resonated with any of the ideas here, that is fine. If you believe that we are living in a world that is progressively getting better instead of worse, how are any of us going to change your mind? If you are proud of what you will be handing down to future generations, then I doubt any argument we could make will successfully shift you from your point of view. Perhaps this book isn't for you. If that is the case, could I persuade you to simply pass it on?

If you refuse to even do that, are you fearful of what might happen should this book find a world-wide following? Could I challenge you to ask yourself why you might feel that way? If not, allow me to suggest that you possess an intolerant and judgmental perspective about things. Or you have chosen to place your own well-being above the well-being of the planet. Where do you plan to spend all that money if we can't start to change some of this stuff?

Ask yourself why, or even how, your mind might be closed to some of these ideas. Ask yourself how you are possibly being manipulated. The answers might enlighten you. In no way has this book demanded anything of any of you. You have only been asked a bunch of questions whose purpose is to encourage you to think.

If you have made it to this sentence, there must be some amount of tolerance within you. Remember, this thing was not professionally written. Perhaps if it was, more of you might have made it this far. Hopefully, some of these ideas have resonated with you. My hope is that you are motivated to initiate some change in the world around you. It will be no small task. But it will be worth the effort.

This book is purposely short. We are at a potential turning point in our collective histories. There is no room for wasted time. Are you overwhelmed by a feeling that these ideas need to be shared as soon as possible? Are we not ready or even eager to discuss and explore them? When you are finished with the book, and if you are so inclined, share it with your fellows. Change must start somewhere. Why not let that change start with you?

The perspectives have been simplified here for no other reason than to make this a shorter read. Books have been written about many of them. There could be many more. I encourage you to read them all. Or even better, write one yourself!

If this book finds an audience, perhaps they will help to expand upon the ideas contained within. I'm hoping that you will be the one to promote some of these ideas.

We need a symbol for change that we can all get behind. Why not let that symbol be a book? We have certainly used them before.

Millions among you are already living by these principles. You will be our guides. We must bring people together with a common purpose in mind. Where this journey might take us will only be limited by our imaginations. It is beyond time that we start having some of these discussions on a global scale. What the fuck have we been thinking?

Start by engaging in whatever you find that enriches your own spirit. Dance, sing, write, pray, hike, exercise, read, meditate, take yoga, or make wonderful artwork. Surround yourself with people who inspire you. Then set out to extend kindness to your fellow human beings. Start talking. Be tolerant. Start to question your leaders, and start thinking about what you want your society to look like. Start changing your world!

On one hand we should have incredible hope. We should believe that we can change. We must believe that there is a future for our children—a future we can be proud of creating for them. On the other hand, we might find ourselves overwhelmed with fear. The only thing that should truly scare us is that future generations might one day discover this book in the ashes of our own destruction. What if the only question they ask of us is... why the fuck didn't we even try?

Appendix

Fear

Scared	Anxious	Nervous	Insecure
Inferior	Threatened	Rejected	Terrified
Helpless	Excluded	Inadequate	Overwhelmed
Worried	Horrified	Persecuted	Exposed
Mortified	Dreadful	Enraged	Exasperated
Worthless	Weak	Hysterical	Frightened
Insignificant	Bewildered	Discouraged	Confused
Foolish	Embarrassed	Submissive	Tense
Frozen	Quiet	Unwanted	Tender
Bored	Stressed	Pressured	Absent

Anger

Enraged	Exasperated	Frustrated	Annoyed
Revolted	Mad	Aggressive	Critical
Hostile	Contemptuous	Hurt	Irritated
Envious	Disgusted	Jealous	Resentful
Aggravated	Numb	Hateful	Selfish
Skeptical	Sarcastic	Distant	Furious

Love

Tender	Longing	Peaceful	Sentimental
Attractive	Intimate	Secure	Romantic

Desirous	Nurturing	Grateful	Trusting
Thoughtful	Content	Relaxed	Caring
Infatuated	Enchanted	Tranquil	Satisfied
Compassionate	Serine	Thankful	Grateful
Enthralled	Loving	Responsive	Relaxed
Spiritual	Enamoured	Open	Sexy

Sadness

Shameful	Bored	Lonely	Melancholic
Disappointed	Isolated	Guilty	Anguished
Powerless	Ashamed	Stupid	Inferior
Regretful	Distressed	Neglected	Displeased
Dismayed	Hurt	Agonized	Hopeless
Sorrowful	Depressed	Apathetic	Remorseful

Happiness

Optimistic	Excited	Stimulating	Cheerful
Proud	Joyful	Hopeful	Eager
Playful	Thankful	Content	Amused
Delighted	Zealous	Rapturous	Jubilant
Illustrious	Triumphant	Pleased	Euphoric
Touched	Elated	Enthusiastic	Enchanted
Respected	Valuable	Worthwhile	Confident
Faithful	Aware	Appreciated	Successful
Important	Discerning	Creative	Energetic
Sexy	Fascinated	Extravagant	Ecstatic

Fulfilled	Inquisitive	Respected	Friendly
Sensitive	Courageous	Fulfilled	Interested

Surprise

Awe-Struck	Amazed	Confused	Disillusioned
Startled	Energetic	Perplexed	Stunned
Astonished	Speechless	Astounded	Shocked
Overcome	Moved	Eager	Dismayed
Touched	Stimulated	Excited	Uncomfortable
Unclear	Dizzy	Fascinated	Engaged

Let's Get the Conversation Started

Website: whatthefuckarewethinking.com

CPSIA information can be obtained
at www.ICGtesting.com
Printed in the USA
LVHW010856090621
689685LV00006B/1100

9 780228 852551